Queen Victoria

Queen Victoria

By Robert Green

A First Book

FranklinWatts
A DIVISION OF GROLIER PUBLISHING
New York London Hong Kong Sydney
Danbury, Connecticut

Photographs ©: Mary Evans Picture Libary: cover, 53; The Bridgeman Art Library: cover, 29, 10, 13, 15, 17, 31, 32, 35, 39, 47, 52; Topham Picture Source: cover, 3, 6, 20, 23, 26, 40, 51, 55; UPI/Corbis-Bettmann: cover, 9, 12, 24, 36, 43, 44, 46, 49, 57;

Visit Franklin Watts on the Internet at:
http://publishing.grolier.com

Library of Congress Cataloging-in-Publication Data

Green, Robert, 1969–
Queen Victoria / by Robert Green.

p.   cm.—(A First book)
Includes bibliographical references and index.
Summary: A biography of the nineteenth-century queen who ruled Britain longer than any other monarch.
ISBN 0-531-20330-1
1. Victoria, Queen of Great Britain, 1819-1901—Juvenile literature. 2. Great Britain—History—Victoria, 1837-1901—Juvenile literature. 3. Queens—Great Britain—Biography—Juvenile literature. [1. Victoria, Queen of Great Britain, 1819-1901. 2. Kings, queens, rulers, etc. 3. Women—Biography.] I. Title. II. Series.
DA557.G75   1998
941.08′092—dc21
[B]   97–10990
                                                                                CIP
                                                                                 AC

Contents

Balmoral Castle, Queen Victoria's favorite residence, lies nestled in the valley of the Dee River in the Scottish Highlands.

I

BEHIND PALACE WALLS

On a crisp morning in September 1860, two Scotsmen named Brown and Grant led a party of four on an excursion into the Highlands of Scotland. The party traveled in a simple manner. They forded streams, wove their way through thick brambles, and climbed rugged hills. The Scottish highlands have always been rough terrain, but its somber beauty enchanted that party of travelers.

So as not to be recognized, the party gave assumed names at local inns and homely taverns. For this was no ordinary party, but Britain's own Queen Victoria and her husband Albert. The queen described their "Great Expedition" as "the pleasantest and most enjoyable expedition I ever made." To be away from politics in London, to be in the open air and among simple people, to be with Albert—these were the things Queen Victoria loved best.

Even with false names, everyone recognized them— this was half the fun. "We had decided to call ourselves Lord and Lady Churchill and Party," she wrote in her diary. "Brown once forgot this and called me 'Your Majesty' as I was getting into the carriage, and Grant on the box once called Albert 'Your Royal Highness,' which set us off laughing."

There was, however, an underlying seriousness to the queen's games. She knew from an early age what it meant to be alone and not to be able to move freely in her own country. Though she enjoyed her travels, Victoria never lost sight of the seriousness of her role as queen. But she brought simple virtues back to a crown tarnished by vice and indifference. By the end of her reign, she had so firmly stamped her age with her personal character that it has been called the Victorian Age ever since.

Victoria was born on May 24, 1819, and christened Alexandrina Victoria. She was simply called "Drina" as a

Edward, Duke of Kent, Victoria's father, had a reputation as a ruthless military commander. He led the royal fusiliers in Canada, and Prince Edward Island was named in his honor in 1799.

child. The royal family in the generations before hers was quite large. So how did Drina become heir to the throne?

Victoria's grandfather, King George III (reigned 1760–1820), who was king during the American War of Independence, had fifteen children—no shortage of sons to inherit the throne after him. When he suffered from madness in his later years, his oldest son became regent, or king in all but name. When George III died in 1820, his son became King George IV.

George IV and his wife, Caroline of Brunswick, had only one child, Charlotte, who married Leopold, the prince of Belgium. There was no one to inherit the throne of England directly, so three of George's brothers scrambled to secure their own families—the Dukes of Clarence, Kent, and Cambridge all married in 1818.

The Duke of Kent, Prince Edward, was Victoria's father. In order to establish a family, he abandoned his French mistress and married Victoria Mary Louisa, a princess from the German state of Saxe-Coburg and a widow with one child, Feodore. Ever since the time of

Kensington Palace became the home of Edward, Duke of Kent, his new wife, Princess Mary Louisa Victoria, and their daughter, Victoria. Edward died shortly after Victoria was born, and Victoria sorely missed his guidance.

George I (reigned 1714–1727), the British royal family was descended from German stock.

The Duke of Kent and his new Duchess returned to England and set up a home at Kensington Palace, which in that day was beyond the hustle and bustle of London's center. Princess Victoria was born shortly after their arrival. "Take care of her," the Duke told the Duchess, "for she will one day be Queen of England." The Duke then promptly died, leaving the eight-month-old Victoria fatherless.

Victoria spent her childhood in the austere rooms of Kensington Palace. Her mother described her as "a pretty little princess as plump as a partridge." Others thought she resembled her grandfather George III. She had the same giant watery eyes, unblinking stare, and tufts of fair hair.

To protect her from anyone who might want to influence her politics, Victoria was denied the friendship of children her own age, with the exception of her half-sister, Feodore, who was her nursery companion and lifelong friend. Victoria later described this time as "a rather melancholy childhood." When Victoria was five, a governess was hired from Coburg. Louisa (later Baroness) Lehzen became the princess's constant companion, and only a very few days of her childhood were spent beyond the watchful eye of either her mother or Lehzen.

German was the principal language of the household, so tutors had to be summoned to teach Victoria English. Her maternal uncle, Prince Leopold, was consulted. He not only arranged for her study of languages, history, dancing, music, and geography, but he also became her principal tutor, sending a constant stream of letters from his home.

Victoria excelled at languages. Aside from her native German, she learned to read and speak French and English, though she never quite mastered Latin (the language of the ancient Romans). Her favorite author as a

Victoria's uncle Leopold in many ways took the place of her missing father. Although Leopold left England to become the first king of the Belgians, he retained a strong interest in Victoria's progress.

child was the Scotsman Sir Walter Scott. Victoria had a quick mind and developed a "fearless straight forwardness," a stubborn streak, and a quick temper. Even at an early age she was learning the power of will.

Leopold was one of the few men Victoria knew well as a child, and she became devoted to him. She visited him as often as her mother would allow and took his advice on every question. "He is indeed like my real father," she said, "for I have none."

In 1831, when Victoria was eleven, Leopold left England to become the first king of the Belgians. Victoria missed her uncle sorely, and they wrote many letters to each other. Leopold suggested to Victoria's tutor that she not be told until later that she would become queen—the children of her father's older brothers had all died in infancy, so Victoria was heir apparent. It became a difficult secret to keep because she was learning about the history of the monarchy and the position of her relatives to the throne.

Eventually, the subject could be avoided no longer. When she was thirteen, Victoria learned her fate, to which she replied with humility, "I will be good." This may seem a simple statement, but it became a celebrated remark in Britain. The reputation of the monarchy during Victoria's childhood had fallen very low. The British, growing weary of selfish and greedy kings, had begun to consider abolishing the monarchy and creating a republic in Britain.

The accession, therefore, of eighteen-year-old Victoria upon the death of King William IV on June 20, 1837, was greeted with much relief.

King William IV had ten illegitimate children, and the two daughters by his wife died in infancy, so upon his death the crown passed to his niece, Victoria.

Surely, thought the English, one so young and so full of good intentions will not rule as the cynical and greedy old men before her had. Victoria was certainly not greedy. It was significant that one of her first acts as queen was to settle all of her father's debts, an act that won great admiration from her subjects, especially the politicians.

Her first appearance at an official Council meeting, where she was introduced to members of Parliament, the governing body of Great Britain, created a sensation. She had been so secluded as a child that few knew what to expect. The grace and dignity with which she carried herself, and the high, clear voice with which she spoke, brought out a flush of patriotism and admiration in even the most cynical old politicians.

A strong streak of Romanticism ran through the Victorian Age, and Victoria's accession unleashed speculation of a new and wonderful age of progress and greatness for England. Lytton Strachey, an English biographer, summed up the feeling nicely: "The nasty old men, debauched and selfish, pigheaded and ridiculous . . . had all vanished like the snows of winter, and here at last, crowned and radiant, was the spring."

Victoria was invested with the symbols
of state, the crown and scepter, during
her coronation on June 28, 1838.

II

Into the Light

The change in Victoria's life—when she stepped over the threshold at age eighteen from her cloistered childhood to the highest position in the realm—could not have been more dramatic. Gone was the constant companionship of her mother and Lehzen. Gone, too, was the desire to be among society where things really happened. Suddenly, England's most powerful men knelt at her feet waiting to please the new queen. "I never was happy," she later recalled, "until I was eighteen."

Yet some feared that she was too inexperienced to rule alone. "Poor little Queen!" wrote one government minister. "She is at an age at which a girl can hardly be

Because Victoria had been raised far from the public
eye, few knew what to expect from the new queen.
Not only did her grace make a great impression
on the public, but her interest in the details of
public affairs impressed government ministers.

trusted to choose a bonnet for herself; yet a task is laid upon her from which an archangel might shrink." But far from shrinking from her new life, Victoria threw herself into it with zeal.

For some time, Victoria's relations with her mother, the Duchess of Kent, had been strained. Her mother was domineering and she wished to control every aspect of Victoria's life. Upon her accession, Victoria made it clear that the duchess was to play no part in ruling Britain. A similar message was sent to her uncle Leopold, who had some hopes of controlling the foreign policy of England through his niece. Victoria had realized the dangers of working too closely with Leopold: Not only would it make her unpopular with her subjects, but it would almost certainly breach the laws of the English constitution. So Leopold, king of the Belgians, was firmly told to limit his letters to personal matters.

Another result of Victoria's accession was an end to the long connection between England and Hanover, the region of Germany that was the home of George I. For 123 years, the crown of Hanover had been passed down with the English crown. But under the terms of the Salic Law, which most of Europe recognized, a woman could not inherit the throne. This law was not in effect in England, but it was in Hanover. Therefore, when Victoria became queen, the Hanoverian throne passed to her

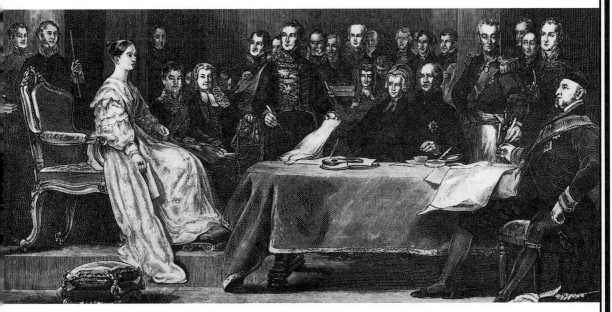

The queen's first council with government
ministers, held at Kensington Palace in 1837,
left even the most cynical politicians cheered
by the promise of youth and virtue.

uncle Ernest Augustus, the duke of Cumberland.

So Victoria was free from unwanted family counsel
and from obligations to Hanover. She turned her attention solely toward the task of governing Britain. "So many
communications from the Ministers, and from me to
them," she wrote, "and I get so many papers to sign every
day, that I have always a *very great* deal to do. I *delight*
in this work." But Victoria was a true novice in politics. She
soon found, in prime minister William Lamb, Viscount
Melbourne, an excellent teacher and a devoted friend.

William Lamb, Viscount Melbourne, had been shunned by King William IV, but he proved to be a valuable counselor and mentor to young Queen Victoria.

Melbourne was something of a puzzle. He was fifty-eight years old at the time of Victoria's accession and had been prime minister for three years. His upbringing was graced with considerable fortune and he entered politics with ease. His wit was celebrated in political circles; so, too, was his melancholy mood, for he suspected that life was really rather pointless.

"The paradox of his political career was no less curious," wrote Lytton Strachey. "By temperament an aristocrat, by conviction a conservative, he came to power as the leader of the popular party, the party of change." This was the Whig party, one of the two major parties in the British Parliament; the other party was the Tory, or Conservative, party.

Melbourne believed that little good could be done by politicians and that it was better to leave things alone. He often uttered sentiments that only one as popular as he could say without damaging his reputation. "You had better try to do no good," he once said.

Victoria, however, brought out a wistful and romantic side of Melbourne. He proved to be a perfect courtier, making the new queen feel like a queen. He was also responsible for Victoria's understanding of the English constitution and the history of English politics. He replaced Uncle Leopold as Victoria's tutor in politics. Through his efforts, the world-weary old man briefly found the rosy glow of youth rekindled, and his steps became more buoyant.

Victoria settled quickly into a daily routine during which Melbourne was usually near at hand. In the morning, she attended to her pile of official communications and was briefed by Melbourne. In the afternoon, a quaint little party of courtiers, including Melbourne, went riding in the countryside. At dinner, Melbourne sat by the queen's side. Sometimes they talked politics, and sometimes he gave entertaining lectures on the history of England.

No monarch could have wished for a more considerate or well-informed prime minister, yet their relationship had one dangerous result: Victoria began to favor the Whig party. The British constitution speaks clearly on this matter. The sovereign must remain detached from party politics, never showing favor to one party over the other. The members of Parliament are elected, and the sovereign must consider the elected ministers, from either party, her own government and show it full support.

The problem became clear in May 1839 when Lord Melbourne resigned and the Conservative party came to power under the leadership of Sir Robert Peel. It was inevitable that Victoria and Melbourne would be separated at some point, but the two resisted with all their hearts. "Flesh and Blood cannot stand this!" sighed Melbourne.

The incident of the Ladies of the Bedchamber brought out all the queen's favoritism of the Whigs. When the queen acceded the throne, Melbourne had surrounded her with Whig attendants. The Mistress of the Robes and the Ladies of the Bedchamber—all queen's servants—were chosen by Melbourne. When Peel took office, he tried to replace them with Tories. The queen's disgust at the thought of being surrounded by Tories erupted into a public scandal.

When Sir Robert Peel became leader of the Conservative Party in 1839, Melbourne and Victoria feared he would try to run affairs in Parliament and in Victoria's life. This political cartoon depicts him as a stage manager listing all the "players" in Parliament he felt he could direct.

The queen refused the change outright, despite the pleadings of Melbourne, who told her that Peel had the right to make some changes as the new prime minister. Peel refused to take office with a queen hostile to him, and Melbourne resumed as prime minister. There is no doubt that Victoria's actions were unconstitutional and the result of her inexperience. Later she would become fond of some Conservative leaders and the entire incident would be regretted.

Oddly enough, Victoria regretted much from her delightful first few years in office. The whirl of parties, the late nights, the sheer exuberance, were contrary to the character of the later queen. "It was the least sensible and satisfactory time in her whole life," Victoria later wrote (referring to herself in the third person, as monarchs do). "That life of mere amusement, flattery, excitement, and mere politics, had a bad effect on her naturally simple and serious nature. But all changed after '40."

Victoria had steadfastly refused any talk of marriage, refusing to share power in the first years of her reign. Melbourne tried to convince her of the virtues of marriage, but it can be tough to convince the young. Melbourne's departure from office was more convincing. "I am a person who has to cling to someone," wrote the queen, "in order to find peace and comfort." And in October 1839, Victoria's views on marriage underwent a complete revolution with the arrival of a young German prince named Albert.

Albert, the comely young prince from Saxe-Coburg-Gotha, arrived at the English court on a visit on October 10, 1839. Just five days later, Victoria proposed to him.

III

LIFE WITH ALBERT

In 1836, Prince Albert, nephew of Victoria's uncle Leopold and Victoria's first cousin, visited England. "Allow me to tell you," Victoria wrote to Leopold, "how much I like him in every way. . . . [H]e has, besides, the most pleasing and delightful exterior and appearance."

Sometime after Victoria wrote those words, Leopold began trying to bring the two together. In 1839, Albert was about to make another passage to England, and Victoria, enjoying her freedom too much to think of marriage, was quite nervous about how to handle him.

Victoria sometimes unleashed a fierce temper
and suffered from depression during the time
that she was raising a young family, but through
it all she took comfort in Albert's presence.

As late as April of that year, she had told Lord Melbourne,
"my feeling is quite against ever marrying." And she
wrote to Leopold, whose schemes she had begun to
resent, "there is no engagement between us."

Three days after Albert arrived in October 1839, though, the queen was smitten. She spoke longingly of his "exquisite nose, delicate mustachios and slight but very slight whiskers," and "the beauteous figure, broad in the shoulders and a fine waist."

She told Lord Melbourne that she had "a good deal changed her opinion as to marrying." Within a week they were engaged, and Victoria had surrendered her entire being to Albert. They were married in February 1840.

Albert drew Victoria away from her youthful enthusiasm for politics and the gay life of London parties. In 1840, their first child, Victoria the Princess Royal, was born. Over the next ten years eight more children would follow (Edward, Alice, Alfred, Helena, Louise, Arthur, Leopold, and Beatrice). Victoria fell into the role of devoted mother and dutiful public figure with surprising grace. She was becoming a symbol of virtue and dignity, restoring a respect for the crown that had eluded her predecessors.

While the public grew to like the queen more and more, Albert received a rather cooler reception. His clipped German accent and stiff manner rubbed many Britons the wrong way. Albert was rigid about decorum and morality, causing an air of stuffiness to hang about the royal court. He became the butt of jokes among England's wealthy aristocrats. They were most offended by two factors: Albert's indifference to sport (although he rode horses and fenced well), and his studious nature.

In addition, Albert had been accompanied to England by an elusive and powerful figure named Baron Stockmar. Stockmar had been a longtime adviser and confidant of Leopold's. Leopold had sent him to England to guide Albert's entry into the world of politics.

Albert's role as the husband of the queen was undefined, and much attention followed his activities. Victoria was determined to keep him entirely on the sidelines, but as she fell under his sway, she relied more and more on his political judgments as well. Stockmar proved to be a brilliant political counselor and tutor on the English constitution, and Albert's intellect proved to be formidable. It was only natural that Victoria should come to rely on his advice.

During Victoria's first pregnancy, Albert began reading state papers. He became, in effect, her private secretary and "permanent minister." Albert also reorganized the royal household, reducing costs and making things run more efficiently.

When Albert negotiated a compromise on the question of the Ladies of the Bedchamber, Victoria was thrilled. Moreover, Albert generally liked Sir Robert Peel. When the Conservatives were voted into power, Albert

Albert held Victoria's unwavering devotion, but he struggled to win the favor of England's public. They saw him as a rigid figure who involved himself perhaps too much in the queen's affairs.

worked a reconciliation between Peel and the queen. (Victoria later developed a fondness for Peel and came to prefer the Conservatives to the Whigs.)

Albert had now proven himself, in the queen's opinion, worthy in all quarters. Victoria later claimed that these days with Albert were the happiest of her life. The royal couple developed a dislike for London and soon purchased two country estates to escape the sooty spires of the capital. One house, called Osborne, was built on the Isle of Wight and the other at Balmoral in the Highlands of Scotland.

Queen Victoria had a lifelong love of the Scottish Highlands. While there, she came to know the Highlander John Brown, who became her favorite servant and constant companion. The distance to Balmoral, however, proved to be a constant nuisance for the queen. To speed the journey, Victoria and Albert began to make the trip on the railway. Train travel had only begun in 1830, but new lines were laid quickly and the steam engine became a symbol of Victorian Britain.

Perhaps the only member of the queen's party who hated the new machines was the Master of the Horse, who was responsible for making the arrangements, previously by horse-drawn carriage, for the royal journeys. On Victoria's first railway journey in

The train carriage that the royal family took
to the Scottish Highlands represented the
height of luxury travel. More importantly, it
symbolized the technological advances
of England's Industrial Revolution.

1842, the Master of the Horse insisted on mounting
the engine and aiding the driver. His court attire of
scarlet livery was blackened by the breath of the new
mechanical beast.

The sprawling Crystal Palace housed the
Great Exhibition of 1851. This view shows
the approach to the Prince's Gate.

Improvements in industrial technology played a
large part in the life of Victorian Britain. The Industrial
Revolution had begun much earlier in Britain than in
most of Europe. By Victoria's time, the British were reap-
ing its fruits.

Sir Robert Peel grasped the importance of Britain's
technological advances and hatched a plan for a cele-
bration that resulted in the Great Exhibition of 1851.

He invited Albert to make all the arrangements, and the prince began to dream up the most enormous and wonderful display of machinery, inventions, and arts.

It proved to be a task for which Albert was born. He pressed all of his love of detail and organizing toward the Exhibition. He chose Joseph Paxton to design an enormous glass structure called the Crystal Palace in London's Hyde Park to house the exhibits. The Great Exhibition opened on May 1, 1851. More than six million people visited during the six months that it was open.

The queen joined the throngs of awestruck visitors in touring the exhibits under the sprawling glass canopy. At one point, after a prayer by the Archbishop of Canterbury, the highest official of the Church of England, a choir sang the "Hallelujah Chorus." While the voices shook the glass panels of the structure, a Chinese man in traditional mandarin costume solemnly approached the queen and bowed.

The queen accepted his flattery as though it were expected. It was discovered later that no representative from China was among the many foreign ambassadors. Many believed that he was an impostor. Victoria would not have agreed, for that would be below her view of the perfection of the moment. It was, she wrote, "the greatest day in our history, the most beautiful and imposing and touching spectacle ever seen, and the triumph of my beloved Albert."

The Exhibition was for Victorian Britain an expression of the feeling of optimism, progress, and security of that age. For Victoria it was another example of Albert's greatness. Many Britons, however, remained skeptical of Albert's patriotism. In a number of scraps with Parliament, Albert advised Victoria, and it became clear that his interpretation of the English constitution was not the same as Parliament's.

Albert tirelessly counseled Victoria to be a firm and active monarch. He warned against allowing her ministers to act too independently, especially in foreign policy, which Victoria tried to control directly. Not surprisingly, many members of Parliament resented Albert's influence, for it reduced their power.

The question of Albert's loyalty was finally put to the test when Britain went to war against Russia in the Crimea (now in the Ukraine) in 1853. Albert and Victoria threw themselves entirely into the war effort. Victoria visited the wounded and instituted a medal, the Victoria's Cross, to honor them. By war's end in 1856, Albert's reputation had been completely vindicated by his tirelessly patriotic efforts on behalf of Britain. War in

"The Charge of the Light Brigade," in the Crimean War's Battle of Balaklava, was actually the result of a tactical blunder by British commanders. Alfred, Lord Tennyson's poem of that name described the charge of the 600 cavalrymen on entrenched batteries of Russian artillery as a heroic action. Less than 250 men survived.

British history has often caused a rise in the popularity of the crown, and the Crimean War was no exception. Victoria and Albert were wildly popular.

Albert had gone through many trials as Victoria's husband, and finally it seemed that he had triumphed. But the queen was not so happy. Albert's health had been declining for some time, and he died on December 14, 1861, probably of typhoid fever.

Victoria demanded that her children share in her
prolonged mourning of Albert. Here, Victoria and
her oldest daughter, then Empress of Germany,
gaze at a portrait of their beloved Albert.

IV
LIFE
WITHOUT
ALBERT

The death of Albert marked a central turning point in the life of Queen Victoria. Her nature and her outlook were forever changed. She wrote that she was left only "a pleasureless and dreary life." She went on, "Oh! to be cut off in the prime of life is too awful, too cruel!" It was, in the words of Victoria's favorite poet, Alfred, Lord Tennyson, "sorrow's crown of sorrow."

From that day forward it was a rare day when the queen did not don the heavy black dress of mourning. She was determined that Albert was never to be forgotten. She commissioned statues to be cast in his likeness and gave public buildings his name. She wished for the entire country to grind to a halt and join her in remembering and mourning Albert.

No longer did the queen wish to live or to rule. She shrank from her public duties and entered an obscure and pathetic period. "I am anxious to repeat one thing," she wrote, "and that one is my firm resolve, my irrevocable decision . . . that his wishes—his plans—about everything, his views about every thing are to be my law!"

She wanted only to live out her final years fulfilling wishes that Albert probably would have wanted and to rule in his memory, in his spirit. She longed to meet him in the Christian heaven, where Albert was surely beaming down on his grieving wife.

For the first time in her life, she was without a close adviser. First there was Uncle Leopold, then Melbourne, then Albert. At the time of Albert's death, however, Victoria was only forty-two years old, and more than half of her reign lay ahead.

She receded from public view, and her mourning took on an air of sickness, with doctors being shuttled in and out of the palace. They announced that she was

John Brown, Victoria's plain-speaking Highland guide, did much to bring Victoria out of her deep melancholy after Albert's death.

The somber Queen Victoria, pictured here in regal dress, inwardly delighted at the expansion of the British Empire. Imperialism had many results, but Victoria believed above all that it acted as a civilizing force on the less developed places of the globe.

unfit to carry on with her duties as monarch, that the grief was debilitating.

Albert had counseled Victoria toward more and more involvement with the government. Suddenly, with his death and her withdrawal, there was a vacuum at the top. Public sympathy for the mourning queen began to diminish. Groups eventually emerged that recommended ridding the country of the monarchy.

In 1864, the London *Times* newspaper launched an attack in its pages: "It is impossible for a recluse to occupy the British throne without a gradual weakening of that authority which the sovereign has been accustomed to exert." Victoria was deeply stung by this and viewed such talk as a personal betrayal.

But the role of the British monarch has always been hotly debated. The constitution of Britain is unwritten; it is a collection of hundreds of years of precedent and is extremely difficult to interpret. The monarch serves as the visible symbol of British unity. The monarch embodied the rich history of the land and reminded the Britons that they had been ruled by a sovereign for more than a thousand years.

Victoria's advisers grasped the fact that Victoria would have to be seen by the people if she wanted the monarchy to remain relevant—a symbol can lose its power if it is not seen. But Victoria spent more and more time at Balmoral in Scotland. She rarely visited London, and only occasionally could she be convinced to open the annual parliamentary session, a time-honored role for the monarch.

Slowly Victoria came to see that her duties to her own people had not ended. She would have no other great adviser, but she could rule on her own. "I am determined," she wrote, "that no one person . . . is to lead or guide or dictate to me." Once again the flurry of advice began to fly to her ministers.

By 1880, public mood had begun to shift. Britain's growing overseas empire drew the attentions of British citizens. Queen Victoria also took an interest in the nation's empire. Domestic politics had always bored her, and she felt that the day-to-day squabbles of politicians were beneath her. Foreign policy was a different matter. Victoria was remarkably well-informed about the British Empire. She swelled with pride at the growing importance of the colonies.

England lost the American colonies in the Revolutionary War (The Peace of Paris, signed in 1783, recognized American independence) but had taken control of Canada in 1763. Moreover, the British had settled in Australia in 1788 and the population there was growing. The British competed with the Dutch settlers known as Boers for control of South Africa, while other Europeans claimed colonies in other parts of Africa.

Most importantly, the British crown formally took control of the English settlements in the Indian subcontinent in 1858. India alone gave Victorian Britain cheap materials and a market for British factory goods. So lucrative was India that it came to be known as the jewel in the

While Victorian Britain was marked by stifling morality, the British Empire drew out a curious breed of eccentric adventurers, such as the fiery Captain Sir Richard Francis Burton. He mapped unexplored areas in the Middle East and Africa for the Royal Geographical Society and commanded the expeditions that resulted in the discovery of the source of the Nile River.

crown—the shining example of British imperialism. The opening of the Suez Canal in northeast Africa in 1869 enabled British ships to travel between Britain and India without having to round the African continent.

Victoria regarded India as her personal property, simply stating that it is "all to be mine." The vastness of the British Empire made it more necessary than ever that the British have a solid and regal symbol of unity, and that was the queen. Victoria had finally been drawn out of her cocoon of sorrow by the promise of an Empire.

Her popularity swelled as the British took more and more interest in the colonies. Over time, she came to favor the Conservatives, the party of Empire. Her dislike of the Whigs grew as they proposed

Although Victoria had great sympathy for the working classes and with her "brown" subjects in the Empire, she could never understand why women would give up their traditional roles to play a part in the male-dominated world of politics and economics. Here, a young suffragist agitates for greater equality in London in the 1890s.

many changes that she considered radical and even dangerous. Victoria was never quick to accept change, and many of her reactions reflect her fixed ideas.

Her reaction to the growing support for women's rights is a characteristic example. The number of men who could vote was already increasing—middle-class political involvement grew with the riches of the Industrial Revolution and Empire. But women in Victorian Britain did not have the right to vote and generally held a lower position in society than men. Victoria did not understand the arguments for allowing greater rights for women. She referred to the movement as "mad, wicked folly." "God created men and women different," she wrote, "then let them remain each in their own position."

For the queen, all that was detestable about the Whig party was embodied in one politician, William Gladstone. "The danger to the country, to Europe, to her vast Empire," Victoria wrote about Gladstone, "which is involved in having all these great interests entrusted to the shaking hand of an old, wild, and incomprehensible man . . . is very great!"

Her loathing of Gladstone's liberal policies strengthened her fondness for the Conservative prime minister Benjamin Disraeli, who took office in 1874. Victoria used her powers as queen to support the Conservatives, a

Victoria despised the Liberal politician
William Gladstone, who constantly tried
to endear himself to her and convince
her to return to ceremonial duties.

position that was clearly unconstitutional. But Disraeli,
a novelist and deeply religious man, intrigued Victoria.
They viewed the Empire with a similar zeal. Most of all,
Disraeli knew how to handle Victoria. "Everyone likes
flattery," he wrote, "and when you come to Royalty you
should lay it on with a trowel."

It was Disraeli who secured the passage of a bill in the British Parliament in 1876 that awarded Victoria the title of Empress of India. Victoria gushed with pride at this extravagant honor. It also symbolized the dizzying heights to which her image rose in the later years of her reign.

Gladstone's rival, the thoughtful and complex Conservative politician Benjamin Disraeli, won Victoria's affections by lending her a sympathetic ear—and by securing her the title Empress of India.

V

THE GRANDMOTHER OF EUROPE

The title of Empress applied only to the queen's position in India. But Victoria was so delighted that she often referred to herself as Queen-Empress in Britain. She had come to accept that the happiest days, her days with Albert, had passed but that a glorious new role had been found.

She had become the eldest royal of Europe and was related to most of the remaining royalty. She was also

This political cartoon depicts the queen resolutely sweeping back the tide of support for the Home Rule Bill, which proposed greater religious and political independence for Ireland.

the leader of the vast Empire and of a public who believed more and more in the things she believed in.

There was a snag, however. In 1880, Gladstone was voted back into office. With the fervor of a preacher, he sought to turn back the course of the Empire and let the peoples of the world choose their own destinies. It was undoubtedly a noble sentiment but not one that the queen shared.

Gladstone believed in the Home Rule Bill, which would grant Ireland more independence from the British crown. Ireland had been under British rule for centuries, and the queen shared the sentiments of most Britons that Ireland should remain so. It was not just a backward place, thought Victoria, incapable of governing itself, it was also Catholic. The queen had taken an oath upon succession to the throne to defend the Protestant faith. As the kings and queens before her had done, she took that to mean no greater freedom for Catholics.

Gladstone was also blamed for not doing enough about the gruesome slayings known as the Phoenix Park murders which terrified London. Crime in Victorian Britain had become the staple of the daily newspapers. Many newspapers and magazines were started during this time, and suddenly the general public could follow Victoria's activities closely through the press. But they could also follow the lurid details of city crime. It was not that London was more violent than in times past, but people read about crime and violence every day.

The *Illustrated Police News of London* was the most popular periodical of the Victorian Age. It was perhaps only a matter of time before a popular hero could shed the light of reason on London's seedy underworld of crime. That figure appeared in the *Strand* magazine

The *Illustrated Police News* fed the public's appetite for lurid details of the seamy, violent underside of London. This early form of tabloid journalism caused a boom in newspaper readership.

in the form of Arthur Conan Doyle's fictional sleuth, Sherlock Holmes.

The public also followed a gripping story of another kind. The British colonial government in Egypt had gotten itself into a jam in the Sudan, just south of Egypt. A messianic Islamic firebrand called the Mahdi had whipped his followers into a frenzy, and they attacked the foreign invaders.

The Mahdi's spear-wielding Sudanese close in on Governor Gordon on the steps of the government building at Khartoum. Gordon was posthumously awarded the title Gordon of Khartoum.

The British were besieged by the Mahdi's forces at the city of Khartoum on the Upper Nile. Gladstone felt that he would be playing the imperialist if he sent troops to reinforce Khartoum. He dithered, and the situation grew increasingly tense. The celebrated and eccentric General Charles Gordon was called in to sort out the problem without an invasion.

Gordon sent a flurry of letters to England requesting support. Queen Victoria flew into a rage, demanding that Gladstone relieve Khartoum and squash the impudent Mahdi. When Gladstone finally acted, it was too late. The Mahdi's forces overran Khartoum, slaughtering the British to a man. General Gordon died in January 1885 on the steps of the government building, firing his last bullets and swinging wildly with his saber at the hordes of Sudanese warriors.

The public followed the tragedy in the papers, and opinion turned strongly against Gladstone's government. Victoria publicly attacked Gladstone. The final blow was delivered when Gladstone's own party voted against the Home Rule Bill. His government fell in 1885.

The fall of Gladstone's government and the return of the Conservatives marked a much happier time for Victoria. The public and the government now fully backed the queen's imperial aims. She entered into what is known as the "Jubilee Period."

Victoria's Diamond Jubilee procession in 1897
celebrated her sixtieth year as sovereign.

The Jubilees—anniversary celebrations of her reign—of 1887 and 1897 were met by cheering crowds. The Indian regiments of the colonial armies, marching through London's streets in full native dress, especially captured the public's imagination. The British were not only proud to hold a vast Empire, but they were growing rich from colonial trade.

Queen Victoria knew the value of the colonies and sympathized with her foreign subjects. Unlike her reaction to the women's movement, she held quite liberal views in other areas. She hated the class and color prejudice of the British aristocrats. "The Lower classes," she wrote, "are becoming so well-informed—are so intelligent and earn their bread and riches so deservedly that they cannot and ought not to be kept back."

After the Jubilee of 1887, Victoria employed an Indian servant called the Munshi and took up the study of Hindustani, one of the languages of India. Many protested at having this foreign and unknown person so close to the queen, but Victoria did not care. It must have been quite a sight to see the overweight, somber-faced old queen, with her white hair tied in a bun, working away at her official communications while the Munshi stood by in regal Indian dress.

To her last days, although failing in mind and body, Victoria followed the progress of the Empire. In 1899, war

Victoria's enthusiasm for the British Empire concentrated chiefly on India—"the jewel in the crown." In her last years, she was nearly inseparable from an Indian servant known as the Munshi.

erupted between the British and the Dutch Boers for dominance in South Africa. Victoria lived just long enough to learn that the British had gained the upper hand. They would have their route from Cape Town to Cairo—from the top to the bottom of Africa the British flag would fly. With this knowledge, Queen Victoria finally succumbed to old age. She died on January 22, 1901, at age eighty-one.

Victoria was the longest-ruling monarch in British history. Her eldest son would succeed her as King Edward VII. At the time of her death, she had thirty-seven great-grandchildren. Only four days before her death, she was visited by her oldest grandchild, William, Kaiser of Germany (German emperor). Her descendants also ruled in Russia and other countries of Europe.

But not only from her sprawling brood did she earn the nickname "grandmother of Europe." She also gave back to the British monarchy an image of private virtue and public dignity. So great was her presence that Britons and colonial subjects felt that this solid old woman had tenderly raised them through an era of rapid change. The American novelist Henry James captured the mood after Victoria's death with the words, "We all feel a bit motherless today: mysterious little Victoria is dead."

Four generations of royalty posed together in 1897. Victoria was succeeded by: her son, King Edward VII (upper right); her grandson, King George V (upper left); and her great-grandson, Edward VIII, who held the throne for just eleven months in 1936 before abdicating to marry an American named Wallis Simpson.

For More Information

Green, Robert. *King George III*. Danbury, Conn.: Franklin Watts, 1997.

Millar, Delia. *Queen Victoria's Life in the Scottish Highlands Depicted by Her Watercolour Artists*. London: Philip Wilson, 1985.

St. Aubyn, Giles. *Queen Victoria: A Portrait*. New York: Atheneum, 1992.

Williamson, David. *Debrett's Kings and Queens of Britain*. Topsfield, Mass.: Salem House Publishers, 1986.

For Advanced Readers

Cannon, John, and Ralph Griffiths. *The Oxford Illustrated History of the British Monarchy*. New York: Oxford University Press, 1989.

Erickson, Carolly. *Her Little Majesty: The Life of Queen Victoria*. New York: Simon & Schuster, 1997.

Strachey, Lytton. *Queen Victoria*. New York: Harcourt, Brace and Company, 1989. (First published in 1921.)

Weintraub, Stanley. *Victoria: An Intimate Biography*. New York: Truman Talley Books, 1988.

Internet Sites

Due to the changeable nature of the Internet, sites appear and disappear very quickly. Internet addresses must be entered exactly as they appear.

The Yahoo directory of the World Wide Web is an excellent place to find Internet sites on any topic. The directory is located at:
http://www.yahoo.com

The Victorian Web links information about social life, religion, literature, science, politics, and much more during Victoria's reign:
http://www.stg.brown.edu/projects/hypertext/landow/ victorian/victov.html

The Victoria Research Web links you to more advanced resources for studying the Victorian Age, such as library archives, journals, and the work of scholars around the world:
http://www.indiana.edu/~victoria/

The official Web site of the Monarchy in Britain provides a fascinating look at royal life throughout history and today, including additional biographical information about Queen Victoria and other significant monarchs:
http://www.royal.gov.uk./index.htm

Many Web sites and search engines provide information and links on broader topics in history. One example is a Web page called History Resources, a guide to a huge variety of history sites:

http://www.liv.ac.uk/~evansjon/humanities/history/history.html

Kings and Queens of England and Great Britain with Years of Reign

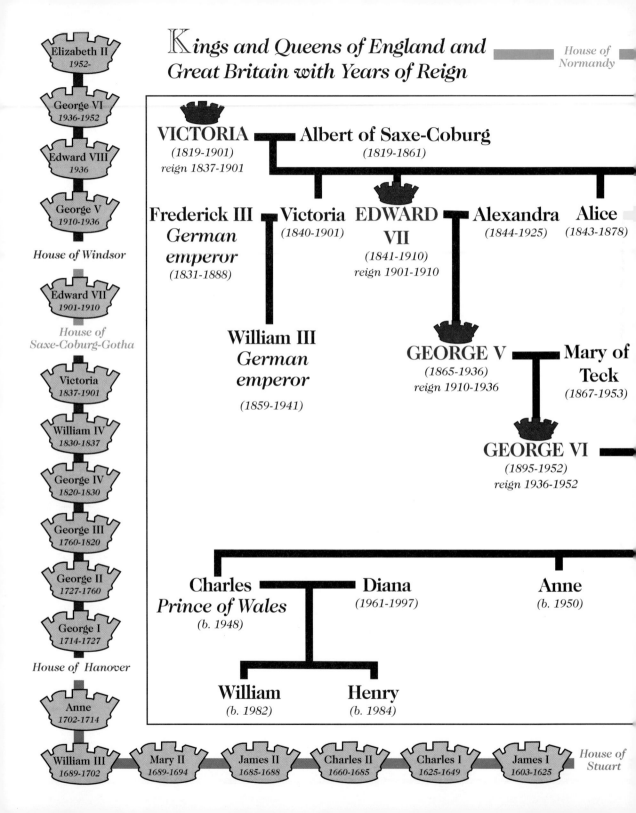

Elizabeth II
1952-

George VI
1936-1952

Edward VIII
1936

George V
1910-1936

House of Windsor

Edward VII
1901-1910

House of Saxe-Coburg-Gotha

Victoria
1837-1901

William IV
1830-1837

George IV
1820-1830

George III
1760-1820

George II
1727-1760

George I
1714-1727

House of Hanover

Anne
1702-1714

House of Normandy

VICTORIA
(1819-1901)
reign 1837-1901

Albert of Saxe-Coburg
(1819-1861)

Frederick III *German emperor*
(1831-1888)

Victoria
(1840-1901)

EDWARD VII
(1841-1910)
reign 1901-1910

Alexandra
(1844-1925)

Alice
(1843-1878)

William III *German emperor*
(1859-1941)

GEORGE V
(1865-1936)
reign 1910-1936

Mary of Teck
(1867-1953)

GEORGE VI
(1895-1952)
reign 1936-1952

Charles *Prince of Wales*
(b. 1948)

Diana
(1961-1997)

Anne
(b. 1950)

William
(b. 1982)

Henry
(b. 1984)

William III
1689-1702

Mary II
1689-1694

James II
1685-1688

Charles II
1660-1685

Charles I
1625-1649

James I
1603-1625

House of Stuart

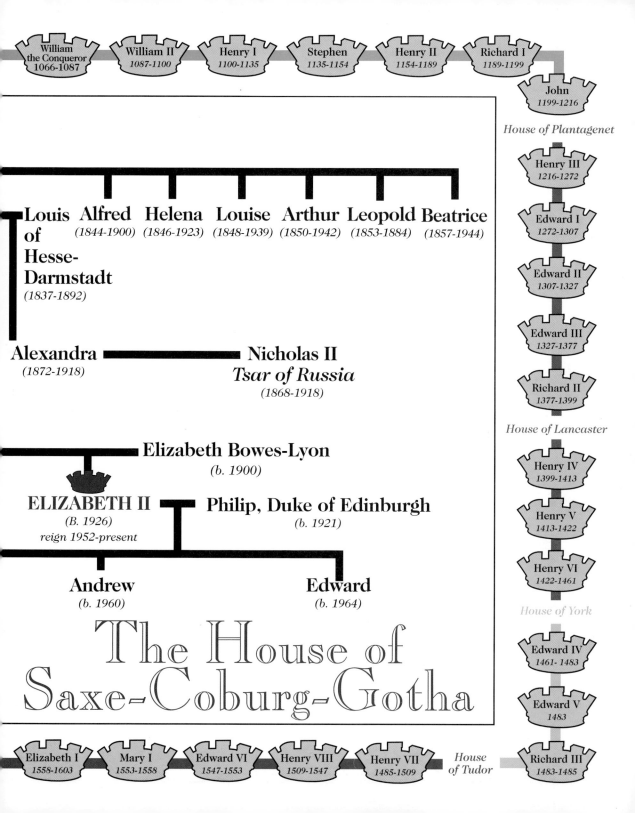

William the Conqueror 1066-1087

William II 1087-1100

Henry I 1100-1135

Stephen 1135-1154

Henry II 1154-1189

Richard I 1189-1199

John 1199-1216

House of Plantagenet

Henry III 1216-1272

Edward I 1272-1307

Edward II 1307-1327

Edward III 1327-1377

Richard II 1377-1399

House of Lancaster

Henry IV 1399-1413

Henry V 1413-1422

Henry VI 1422-1461

House of York

Edward IV 1461- 1483

Edward V 1483

Richard III 1483-1485

Louis of Hesse-Darmstadt *(1837-1892)*

Alfred *(1844-1900)*

Helena *(1846-1923)*

Louise *(1848-1939)*

Arthur *(1850-1942)*

Leopold *(1853-1884)*

Beatrice *(1857-1944)*

Alexandra *(1872-1918)*

Nicholas II *Tsar of Russia* *(1868-1918)*

Elizabeth Bowes-Lyon *(b. 1900)*

ELIZABETH II *(B. 1926)* *reign 1952-present*

Philip, Duke of Edinburgh *(b. 1921)*

Andrew *(b. 1960)*

Edward *(b. 1964)*

The House of Saxe-Coburg-Gotha

Elizabeth I 1558-1603

Mary I 1553-1558

Edward VI 1547-1553

Henry VIII 1509-1547

Henry VII 1485-1509

House of Tudor

Index

Page numbers in *italics* refer to illustrations.

About the Author

Robert Green is a free-lance writer who lives in New York City. He is the author of *"Vive la France": The French Resistance during World War II* and biographies of important figures of the ancient world: *Alexander the Great, Cleopatra, Hannibal, Herod the Great, Julius Caesar,* and *Tutankhamun,* all for Franklin Watts. He is also the author of biographies of other British monarchs: *Queen Elizabeth I, Queen Elizabeth II, King George III, King Henry VIII,* and *William the Conqueror.*